Rendered for More

Rendered for More

Regina Murden

Elm Hill

A Division of
HarperCollins Christian Publishing

www.elmhillbooks.com

Rendered for More

Published in Nashville, Tennessee, by Elm Hill, an imprint of Thomas Nelson. Elm Hill and Thomas Nelson are registered trademarks of HarperCollins Christian Publishing, Inc.

Elm Hill titles may be purchased in bulk for educational, business, fund-raising, or sales promotional use. For information, please e-mail SpecialMarkets@ThomasNelson.com.

Library of Congress Cataloging-in-Publication Data

Library of Congress Control Number: 2020901616

ISBN 978-1-400331109 (Paperback)
ISBN 978-1-400331093 (Hardbound)
ISBN 978-1-400331116 (eBook)

Contents

DEDICATION

I would like to dedicate this book to my family.
Thank you for your support.

Introduction

Have you felt like you were ALL alone, gasping for air, searching for a light to shine through this dark place where you are surrounded by heaviness, deceit, and persecution?

As you remain in this desolate environment, you become suffocated waiting for that light to shine through that dark space you are in, but find out that the light you are waiting to shine or at least flicker for a sign of hope will never occur.

You are all alone in this environment. Yet there is something much deeper within. Outwardly, you are viewed as helpless, surrounded by cantankerous spirits that are giving you a counterfeit identity of being helpless. Each breath becomes shorter by the second as if your throat encloses and all you feel is a dry lump with minimal air passing that keeps your head and sternum in place. HMMM…it is within…yes, within you is where the strength comes minute by minute, second by second, not knowing when this exasperation will end. While internally, something is growing in you despite the distressing atmosphere that sits in your presence, surrounding you in what seems to be an enclosed room that reeks hopelessness and a vile odor you are not familiar with. However, you constrain in this unfitting environment, because it is within you, yes—within where the strength lies.

"What shall I render unto the Lord for all his benefits toward me? I will take the cup of salvation, and call upon the name of the Lord. I will pay my vows unto the Lord now in the presence of all his people."

(Ps. 116:12–14 KJV)

PART 1

Examples of Rendering

CHAPTER 1

Esther's Feet: Unwavering Confidence

"If it scares you, it might be a good thing to try."

— **Seth Godin**

It was the beginning of a new year...school year to be exact. The nerves that subside within me has been stifled by dreams of wonders and soft caresses of my Hello Kitty pillow. As I was partially coming to reality...

Zing! *Uggh.* Zing! My alarm goes off. My stubby hand clumsily reaches over to the device that dictates my moves. Zing! Okay, you win, as one pasty stiff and tingling eye opens. Taking in that last breath and softly sighing, I unwillingly open both of my eyes from a dream state illusion that seem possibly my reality.

I begin to sit up like an iron board that has not been let out yet. A bright yellow light that darts across the room meet the pupils of my dilated eyes before they are ready to welcome any contact to sight. Flinching. The sunlight has blinded my perception of my room. I sit for a while, and ponder if it is today that I embark upon my journey of life or new day of work. I begin to silently reflect upon my successes and my failures. I've always considered myself to be known as having a bondservant relationship with Christ.

- Went to church. Check.
- Prayer. Devotion time. Check.
- Bible Study. Check.
- Community outreach. Check

I considered myself to be one of those servants who is "in tune" with God. All these aspects are wonderful to do for they are good habits. However, it was when my interpersonal life was turned upside down; just when I noticed they were habitual, but not quite intentional HABITS. I guess you could say I am one of those behavior modified Christians. You know, like those good chewy marshmallows on aisle six—the jumbo size. They appear to be pure, smooth, interchangeable for the liking of your preference. However, you notice the marshmallows seem to be slightly bland or hollow.

Well, that was me. Yep, that's right.

It was about 7:15 a.m. when I had a date with discovering my behavior modification tendencies. It was late August; I arrived punting curves to make it in the parking lot. In my little civilized Honda. Screech…! Oh great! What a great first impression to make upon the colleagues. Well, it does not actually count until spoken words partake your mouth…so I was told. I had time to redeem myself. Rushing through the door…acclimate. Acclimate. Acclimate…I calmly tried to look for my mailbox and make it to my room.

I entered a zone that I was not ready to accept. It all began at my job as a teacher. Yes, a TEACHER! I was new on the scene and let's say that "the struggle was real." It was more like the episode of *The Walking Dead*. Everywhere I turned, there seemed to be zombies surfacing. Hence, this was only the first day of school. I felt awkward. The palpitation of my heart began to get faster, and at times it seemed not beating at all. I checked to see if I was alive periodically. I felt like that little kid looking at her mom leaving her at kindergarten for the very first time, not knowing what exactly lies ahead. Except it was the other way around. I was not the student but the teacher…and I still felt my mom has not yet returned and a degree from accredited college has left me hanging.

I asked myself several times, "Am I at the right place for teaching?" Surely not, however deep down, I gave myself a pep talk. "I'm a Christian, therefore, you can do this. How hard could it be? You know the acclaimed scripture, 'I can do all things through Christ who strengthens me'" (Phil. 4:13 NKJV).

Yep there goes some of that behavior modification sipping in at that moment. Better known as the *holiosis*—one who is inflamed with being too holier than thou and can provide the proper Christian mannerism without the intent of really following through.

Anyone else guilty of having this besides me?

Looking around the surroundings upward to the blue sky then downward towards my feet, saying to myself, "Here I am," in my shrill voice….

Well, I walked in the school building ready to give my all and teach. I knew I was the new kid on the block and there would be a test of proving you are worthy of being part of the team. A no-brainer, however, I imagine it would not be an easy terrain at first for I have been through various circumstances that was not cumbersome, but I manage to overcome.

Well, I walked in smiling and greeting, ready to tackle the task that lies ahead. When I smiled or simply said hello in exchange, I received an under the breath voice grunt or the rolling of the eyes. OKAY….

This is not a friendly environment or perhaps a coincidence, it was a bad day for them. I quietly told myself, "I am not taking it personally. I'm the new kid on the block." It wouldn't be easy, well, not at first, so I assumed settling into my classroom.

Well, Vietnam zombie came dashing in just to wish me to have the worst year possible, saying from that day forward, it would be pure hell. Alrighty. Then, persnickety zombie came in not too long afterwards to pretty much boost her ego from my first day jitters.

Finally, I didn't know which way my head was facing zombie…let's just say I did not manage to make it into the room but got a bird's-eye view by casing the perimeters.

My class had arrived. Most were taller than I. Welcoming them with smiles and a friendly greeting. The students were hesitant to speak. Right at that moment, I felt that God had placed me in the wilderness.

I began to think about Esther. She, too, had to walk with the feet of bravery, not knowing exactly where it would lead her precisely. Yet, the wilderness was calling, and she had to be there. In her case, Shushan was Esther's wilderness. She was orphaned. Let alone unlike me who felt like her mom has abandoned her on the first day of school. Nevertheless, she felt her mom abandoned her for life because she did not have an earthly mom or dad. They were dead. However, she followed the calling of her heavenly Father to go and be positioned at Shushan. Whereas Mordecai, her uncle who adopted her, prepared her for her destiny.

Often at times, we must continue to move in the direction of God's guidance just like Esther. We must trust and believe that God is in control of all our certain and uncertain circumstances. We see in the Book of Esther, Queen Vashti was dethroned simply because she did not cater to the innermost ego of King Ahasuerus. Now, Esther had been placed as the queen; a state of royalty. Just imagine moving from being orphaned all your life to being known as royalty. The position was not easy because she had to please a temperamental king who had significant amount of wealth and made her feel uncomfortable. Yet, Esther continued to tread onward to where God was leading her because there was a deliverance for the Jews. Just then, I realized we cannot become fearful of what people may do to us, whether it's your coworker, boss, or family. When God places you in your wilderness, you can be confident in God's control.

My wilderness was a school in what did not seem to be a promising year. I saw that God had literally thrown me into the wilderness to move me from shallowness, in order to reveal my not so pretty layers that lay within. We tend to want to conceal our boo-boos and insecurities. Whereas, that is where our transformation occurs. God no longer wanted me to be orphaned to Him by living a behavior modified Christian life.

Instead, He wanted me to join and embrace my royal ties by no longer living a selfish, modified Christian life. It required more of me to go deeper and trust God with the positioning of my feet. It was in my wilderness where I began to unfold the sacredness of alignment of place. Yes, I screamed inside and outwardly at times at the wilderness of school. I was led here yet it felt dysfunctional, and causing me to lose grip of the little control that I once possessed in my life to surrendering all to God. It was unnatural and heart-wrenching. Yet I have given in thus far, I continued to go step by step into this wilderness. Yes, grief accompanies us during our most fragile state. It is during the wilderness when we feel as if we have run dry; but it is through this vulnerability that we activate our faith that can only replenish us.

We look at the Book of Esther, we see grief is not a stranger when God is in the process of developing circumstances. Here, we see in chapter four of Esther that Mordecai is in a state of grieving. The significance of his state is not in secret but he was openly grieving. I have been there where there is nowhere to hide and all masks are off. It's raw and just plain ugly, and yes at times, I showed up being unkempt. Thus, Mordecai did not struggle with the notion of losing face. Mordecai literally went publicly and took it to the streets. Nowadays, Mordecai would possibly use the social media platform to express his level of grief with a GoFundMe account. Pride was not an issue for Mordecai. He grieved with the leading of his feet to the king's gate. Talk about being extra. However, it is when most (we) come to this state within that we desire more and seek for a better outcome. In Mordecai's position of being led to grieve displayed the desire to return to their God.

When was the last time you have grieved to God openly? Perhaps you have become too secular and it is time to reposition yourself back on the path of protection with God.

Boy, was I scared, so I thought this just might be a good thing!

CHAPTER 2

The Spirit of Esther: Transitions/Priorities (Identity/God Is the Center)

"Great spirits have always encountered violent opposition from mediocre minds."

"My religion consists of a humble admiration of the illimitable superior spirit who reveals himself in the slight details we are able to perceive with our frail and feeble mind."

– **Albert Einstein**

What would your spirit reveal about you? Are you often too quick to over rationalize outcomes? Or are you presumptuous, impatient, and deflect your insecurities on to others? Would others say you are content, admirable, and assured?

The spirit of Esther possessed a hidden jewel that was valuable to reaching her destiny. Although she is known as a woman who affected her reality and made an impact in the world. The uniqueness of Esther being chosen by King Ahasuerus was not about her beautiful face, luxurious locks, or dazzling eyes. Ahasuerus' vulnerability was attracted to the hidden beauty within Esther. The king saw Esther's beauty that carried treasure, not knowing at the time that he was attracted to her inner being.

Esther's spirit was in position to be placed where God would ultimate use her. Therefore, God allowed her internal spirit to be seen. God will often do the same for you when you position your spirit in God's presence. Here, Esther knew her identity as a Jew could not be exposed unto mediocre matters of others as she transitioned into a role of royalty. A queen required much finesse yet alone discreetness since she had not presented her identity to King Ahasuerus until the appointed time. The king only saw the drip of Esther's beauty.

In our lives, God does not reveal our identity, especially during our transitional seasons, until the appointed time. Usually, when we are presented with the task God wants to reveal about ourselves, which require more than we could possibly handle within our own strength, that feeling is exhilarating and overwhelming because we know deep inside there is more and we are the ones who can be the catalyst for change in that environment (gasping for air from an oxygen tank), while no one really recognizes what we see or feel but the ones that are called to our assignment.

Just as we see in Esther's life, she had many who were attracted to her spirit because they are assigned.

Here's the role's call:

Mordecai – Esther's uncle who possessed the power of the court and was a descendant of one of those exiled Jews. He was a godly man, and his most significant role was his relationship to Esther

The seven bondservants – These servants were in close proximity in providing the information needed for Esther's favorable positioning with the king.

The king – His position allowed Esther to be able to set the Jews free.

Shushan (Persia) – Where the location was in.

Vashti – Her beauty and failure to obey the king's order provided insight for Esther to become savvy. Beauty was skin-deep, and she must follow through with the king's order for victory. Vashti's downfall gave led to Esther's entrance.

Haman – The antagonist. His pride and lustfulness led to his own downfall and Esther's victory for the Jews.

All play a significance to Esther becoming known as one of the greatest heroines.

She was considered meek, modest, reserved, having restraints, and being clandestine. Yes, the opposite of how many would categorize a heroine. In today's norms, these are not the qualities that scream becoming known as a GOAT (the greatest of all times). Maybe a SHEEP, which is not considered as dreadful once we place our perspective properly.

Society encourages putting yourself among others. At all times, it is a must because you are important; you should be demanding, have no restraints, and do not conceal yourself. We have become grafted into a society of "Insta" that has encouraged an unhealthy view that we should be filtering our lives, showing only our best selfies that are often portrayed as falsies, because we don't see many expose the process of getting to the current state. The process is frightening, sad, discouraging, confusing, and just not rose colored. Whereas, Jesus Christ has called us to empty ourselves to be filled. We are to show our boo-boos. Heck! I've earned those scars. What makes them less appealing or effective?

The truth. The enemy uses a community-based platform where we can openly be wounded together, yet it is a facade of judgment. Who is doing the judgment? Ironically, ourselves…we spend limitless hours on trying to perfect the right image for others to view us. We already made perfect in God's image. The self-harm we inflict on ourselves is damaging to our most inner core—our spirits.

In life, we become frustrated humans simply because we feel we have been slighted. We become combative to others in our transitions. We begin to remove our hearts from our sleeves and begin to wear that unformidable badge of "Oh, I'll show you…just watch." When in most cases, it is not that you are being overlooked.

Esther understood this principle well by applying to herself seven attributes to develop a spirit rendering for a purpose that is higher than oneself.

Esther's Hidden Attributes

Inner Beauty

Esther used her natural beauty. It was custom that the young women undergo a year of cosmetics and outer beauty modification. Esther denied the services. She simply relied on the strength of her inner beauty to capture King Ahasuerus' attention. Being the best version of yourself always wins.

Confidence

She was aware of her inner power to make a difference for the Jews. She remained hidden until the time was rightfully hers, restraining from boasting about her position.

Depended on God

Even though it was not mentioned once in the Book of Esther, evidence show how she courageously made a stance to give up her last life for the new life to become a queen. Esther's wisdom gave her provision for the salvation of her people with a special relationship with God. Prayer in fasting for repentance brought a miracle that no pleading to a king could ever render.

Leader

To lead or not to lead? Esther took it upon her rightful duty to act to save her people. Often at times, Esther was not always in the front. Esther's leading involves being hidden and being beside the king.

Hopeful

Esther knew the importance of documenting the story for others to read. The story that we know as Purim. Esther wanted a remembrance for Jews and others to know to never give up on hope.

Sacrificial

Esther made a sacrifice by deciding to stand with the Jews. She made her case by saying, "If I perish, I perish." Esther could easily be summoned.

Community

We are better when we work together. Esther knew this concept was evident to overcome the obstacle that lay before them. Esther told her uncle, Mordecai, to gather all the Jews in unity. This is essential when overcoming oppositional forces. Haman was after the Jews and plotted hatred towards the people.

Jesus always will enter our story. He is a father who is willing to deliver us in our personal lives. The confidence that Esther displayed allowed God to release the sovereignty of the protection of the Jews. Just imagine being isolated most of your life, not having any family. She was wrestling with loneliness, sadness, and the sense of belongingness.

Esther did not have a home. She resonated with the treasure she possessed within her heart—the identity that God has given Esther. It is the spirit that determines your identity. The spirit is formed first, then the soul that comprises our thoughts and feelings and the ultimate decision to surrender our will to God. This is the birthing of our identity. It is not through the masses of societal norms where our identity is formed. We are guilty of letting the society decide for us what should make us happy and unhappy. Looking at materialization and not spiritualization, I am guilty of being victimized by this unhealthy mentality.

Esther, given a hardship early in her life, grasped the importance of God's offering. God gives us rest. It is vital that we learn how to let our souls rest. God said if we are overburdened, weary, and torn, we should come to Him and learn how He handled life. Esther did just that by coming to God even through the turbulence of winds that had been blown into her life early on. She grabbed on to the anchor that continuously guided her to her destiny. The destiny was not just for Esther but for all who was attached to the assignment. She radically obeyed what was relayed to her spirit.

Do you take time and ask what is attached to you?

What am I being called to? Is this Spirit led? Or fleshly driven?

We should be intentional, conscientious beings driven for more that beckons outside ourselves, therefore becoming no longer being self-ambitious but seeking what best for humankind.

Esther did that by being placed right before she was positioned as a queen into a harem or lower with other women. She became wise by developing her spiritual character. Most of us in these dire circumstances would do what we know best for ourselves.

Imagine this was a modern-day *The Bachelor* show and only one girl will get the rose. Most ladies doll themselves with the finest perfume, makeup, clothes, and jewelry that society screams, "You are gorgeous and no man would say no to you!" Well, Esther was highlighted in this sort of episode. However, she had been trained spiritually before she was ever casted into this role to be with these beautiful women, hoping to capture not only the eye but the heart of the guy, King Ahasuerus.

Esther's advantage was not her looks. The advantage she had was not because of name-dropping her uncle, Mordecai. The advantage was within—Esther's spirit. She became acquainted with knowing how to heed and submit to the spirit inside her heart.

We tend to ignore that spirit within and seek for the outside contenders that yell for our attention. Esther had become disciplined in this area to know the importance of seeking help—the spirit. Esther acquired wisdom and applied it. We are humans that are consumed by our selfish ambitions, not wanting to give leverage to what could be best for us. Not Esther; she did what the king wanted and not what she wanted to do.

Her beauty alone was not going to give her that final rose. However, the source within positioned her to stand out among her competitors of women. She did not try to do a knockoff Gucci look or the latest hairstyle. She sought for the recent spiritual counsel. In this case, she was led spiritually to Haggai. Haggai was over the women in the house. But because Esther was being led spiritually and not physically, the wisdom to go ask Haggai, the king's servant for specifics, gave her the advantage.

Aha! Haggai was the mantle to Esther's role of being a queen.

Haggai knew exactly what made the king happy. He knew all the right colors, jewelry, perfume, and the way Ahasuerus, the king, liked makeup on women.

Hence, if we look at the reasoning for why the king was selecting a new queen, Vashti—who entailed all the wonders of a beauty can obtain—was dethroned from her position because she did not do what the king wanted her to do. She became enthralled with the title and followed her own pursuits. In life, we tend to be guilty of not yielding to our king—God. God has a greater role in our lives than the minute plans we belly up ourselves.

We are spiritually inclined beings that are created for God's kingdom.

I can remember in my personal journey as a teacher; at the time, looking at this world that is consumed of darkness. But knowing that I am a vessel filled with the light, I have to be fearless to the pressures surrounding me.

Yes, there were more than once a voice or whisper entered my mind saying, *Why contend with these circumstances?* The harsh and unfair treatment became a familiarity that the odor became embedded within my skin. I was captive. I became paranoid; the agony of my situation became an unwanted layer that continuously held me captive.

I would take showers, rub my skin in hopes that the illusion would wash away. It was a heaviness of rebelliousness, despair, and control. All I knew is that it was not welcome here. I could not understand literally why this stench of discomfort became attached to me without my consent. I came to the realization it was the environment. The conditions of this specific place contained toxic, foul yet limited resources that want to devour me. It was a salvage.

Why me? What do I have to offer? Nothing. Not me.

Wrong.

I had enveloped within me a vessel. I heard about vessels. A vessel is *"a hollow container, especially one used to hold liquid, such as a bowl or cask."*

Well, in the spiritual sense. A vessel can be described as formed to contain something which does not materialize externally to the senses, but is of the spirit, of the soul. We are living vessels that are inclined to the spiritual realm.

What makes me under attack is because I am a vessel. I found out to my astonishment the enemy knew more about what I was equipped with than myself. I remember feeling this covering, trying to find its new home on the creases of my muddy skin. Why would anything want to take residence there? Beats me. It was a heaviness which makes me think about, surely Esther must felt this colliding war of the forces surfacing in her personal situation. She was fighting unknown spirits in a room that wanted to prevent her to arrive to her destined place for not just herself but for multitudes of Jews. Yet she prevailed and continued to submit to the greater spirit within than the outsourced spirits.

What could your spirit be combating? Doubt. Hatred. Envy. Malice.

In all honesty, first, I begin to put matters in my own hands; succumbing to the surnames of plan A, plan B, and plan C. Surely, I am not the only one that does this in their lives. I was on a mission to overcome my circumstances. Little to my astonishment, all the plans where void to fighting this new heaviness. I begin to feel vulnerable and naked. I thought to myself, everyone can see me differently now. As I was sitting at my once prized teacher's desk now to a desk I despise deeply, a voice loudly within said, *Vessel!*

Jumping up from my desk, looking to see no one has entered the room. I was checking to see without a doubt I was left in the room with just me and my thoughts.

I became breathless.

At once, I became informed there was a SPACE INVADER. This invader was worse than a leech, as this invader was invisible with high intensity that affected your living existence.

The outsourced spirit would use people within my school-based environment to harm me. Trust me, I am one who does not like to be in anybody's face. I concluded I was under attack. Walking through the solace hall, not capable to voice my words but through my eyes bearing a sign of help! *Help! I'm captive.* Continuing with the daily routine of walking the class to their support classes when I wanted to walk right out of that school building. Yet, I could not because there was much at stake.

We evolve in our predestined environments. Predestined environments are temporary but essential for the maturation of our vessel. I have a vessel, you have a vessel. A vessel is our lifeline to be equipped in this world full of battles, distress, discomforts, and transformations.

These feelings of doubt, insecurity, despair are all disguised masks of the invader. However, at times, we must go to the invader's environment.

Yet I was doing it all wrong. At that moment, I became equipped. We are merely existing only until we accept the call to live. Our vessel links us to our passion, the truth to why we tick. The invader must leave. While others could not see it, but I certainly felt it. The struggle that what once seemed real was not real no longer because I found my identity in the story God was writing for my life. The threats, schemes from the administration, and plots were no longer encompassing my mind. I have been stretched to be guided by my inner spirit for wisdom. Just as Esther had done in her story written in God's identity.

I became a private investigator swiftly by being bold. Walking the halls of the school knowing who I am. I am not the product of the finicky attributes of my counterparts wishing me to fail in a career that is rewarding. I no longer looked at the demises as attacks, but as a springboard to my destiny. I did not reach this revelation until I decided to submit to the spirit within. I knew there was more ahead.

CHAPTER 3

The Ears of Esther: Boundaries/Next Level (Do Not Allow Everything Toxic)

"The ear is the only true writer and the only true reader."

– Robert Frost

Hear ye, hear ye. Have you ever noticed when one gets hold of good information by overhearing or intentionally listening to others, it becomes a portal for communication? Many begin to gossip, pick up the phones and text about the valuable goods they are withholding. Believe it or not, ears play a huge role in our society for multiple purposes. The positioning of the ears play a key role in the assignment that was given to Esther.

Esther had now approached the courtyard of the palace. Just imagine her heart was racing inside while looking at the majestic view of the castle with awe at Shushan. The columns, lions, glazed brickwork, and imposing statues were just breathtaking and quite different from her previous accustomed environment.

Every step Esther took to the palace leading to her new role must had been intensified with the excitement of knowing she had been chosen to be cherished by the king who was also her husband. The transitions Esther encountered required strong faith. She had to be careful not to rely on her sight of the operations in the palace and trust God through the transition.

The king knew nothing of the God Esther served. King Ahasuerus was only accustomed to Persian law. The law that forbade the very thing Esther was assigned to do. Mordecai insisted that Esther remained in silence. Esther positioned her ears in confidence that her uncle's timing would be best.

> *"Mordecai had instructed the girl to be discreet about her Jewish heritage; he no doubt saw that among Persian royalty, there was much prejudice against his people."*
>
> *(Est. 2:10, paraphrased)*

As instructed, Esther remain to her personal affairs without revealing herself as a Jew to her husband in order to maneuver into the king's favor with access to his ear.

Early on, we see that Esther was not only spirit-led. She already became exposed to a powerful tool; her ears could lead her with the right navigation of timing and wisdom to the keys of unlocking success for Jews.

Surely, the king spoke harsh words to Esther. Yet Esther did not misuse the role of being his queen by backbiting. She embraced the power of her ears to read between the lines of what was to come in the near future. She knew that her role as the queen gave her an honorable access to information that would make a difference in the society.

Who knows, perhaps Esther walked to the side enclosed (side note) to herself, murmuring about the unrealistic idiosyncrasies she overheard from the king and his court. I know for sure that sticking out the tongue and an eye roll or two would have been my friends serving in that gigantic palace. But Esther was focused and knew this was not the time to be mindless and childish. Esther was displaying she was trusting God no matter what her blemished surroundings seemed to be exposing. Trust is not as easy to do as to saying, "I choose to trust you, God," at first. It brings animals out of me—I become a zebra, confused, not really knowing my true stripes—am I white or black? Not accepting I am both. It takes all parts of me to make me the unique person God created me to be. The next animal I become acquainted with is the sloth. I can become very lazy at times in my spiritual walk in trusting, simply because I let fear capitalize on the movement God is doing in my life. I am not proud of admitting to my laziness, but it happens. Then, there is the alligator. I am pretending to be calm and collected, and yes, fierce on the outside; but on the inside, I am a wreck, and if you come too close to me, I'm ready to snap. Then God continues to pour out His patient love towards me and tells me to get up and trust me. Yes, I get up and even begin to move in a zigzag running motion like a gazelle. As if I'm saying to God, "You can't catch me, you can't catch me," then pants for air because I have run beyond my measures. Then, I'm ready to truly trust God. Why do I fall into this useless trap of not believing God from the beginning? I know God has my best interest in mind.

Esther became disciplined in this principle. God knew Esther was a woman He could use without wavering in her selfish doubts for the truth that is in our caring—Abba, God. There were no animals to be found bursting through her alter ego. We know that faith comes from the hearing of the Word.

Faith to believe God's Word is the very essence of receiving the promises that He says we can have. As a Christian, the scripture says, "faith cometh by hearing, and hearing by the word of God" (Rom. 10:17 KJV), then what have I been doing with my ears? Have I become deaf? Silencing the true message of God's truth for my life. I read and heard the words... did I believe? Perhaps, I did believe, but what did I do with being exposed to the words? Belief alone is not good enough when God is trying to use you in most cases beyond your capacity. It is a two-step process; believe and act upon the truth God gives you.

Esther did just that; she did not let the words she heard go into one ear and out the other. She positioned herself in humility and trust, knowing that timing was pivotal in transitioning. Our transitional pauses in our lives enable us to use our ears for positioning.

My experience as a teacher left me shattered momentarily. There were many broken pieces to the puzzle, and I found myself exhausted most days. The strategic plots that was schemed by man hands did not actually prevail because I positioned my ears.

Through the unpleasant experiences in an environment that thrive off unhealthy forces, my God led me to hear through my ears to know the proper move to take. In honesty, the uncanny words my ears were able to receive were some difficult ammo. The school building became a walking landmine for my soul. I was beginning to cowardly curl up within myself, thinking for lack of a better word, "How can one be so evil?"

As Esther was going through turbulent times herself where she literally hid her identity in a geographical area known as Persia—let's not forget Persia was definitely unfavorable of the Jews—she had to walk uprightly, smile, and be pleasant when she knew at times the odds looked as if it was against her. She knew without a doubt this was a transitional phase in her story. God was using her for more than her personal growth. God was developing Esther for the assignment and the people who were attached to her purpose.

Until I became not only submissive to the spirit, I also disciplined myself to allow my ears to follow the truth that rely in the word and kept myself blameless. The gossip, untruths, and harsh setups became just white noise to me. I followed suit and suddenly understood this was for a higher purpose.

The significance of ears is not always noticeable on humans. Mostly covered with hair and usually just go unnoticed by our peers, yet they serve as powerful instruments given to us by our God. Diving more into the story of Esther, it is mentioned that she uses her ears as a guide for her spiritual deliverance three times.

The three instances that mention of her using hearing to lead her to a purposeful destiny involve Mordecai, the bondservants, and Haggai.

Mordecai

> *"Esther did not reveal her ethnicity background or her family background, because Mordecai had ordered her not to..."*
>
> *(Est. 2:10 CSB)*

Bondservants

In Esther 4, we see the intricate role that one of the bondservants who led to using the king's official named Hathak that led to the victory. It states:

> *"Esther's male and female attendants came to her. They told her about Mordecai. So she became very troubled. She wanted him to take off his rough clothing. So she sent him other clothes to wear. But he wouldn't accept them. Then Esther sent for Hathak. He was one of the king's officials. He had been appointed to take care of her. She ordered him to find out what was troubling Mordecai. She wanted to know why he was so upset."*
>
> *(Est. 4:4–5 NIRV)*

> *"So Hathak went out to see Mordecai. He was in the open area in front of the palace gate. Mordecai told him everything that had happened to him. He told him about the exact amount of money Haman had promised to add to the royal treasures. He said Haman wanted it to be used to pay some men to destroy the Jews."*
>
> *(Est. 4:6–7 NIRV)*

Haggai

> *"Now when the turn came for Esther the daughter of Abihail the uncle of Mordecai, who had taken her as his daughter, to go in to the king, she asked for nothing but what Hegai the king's eunuch, who had charge of the women, advised. Now Esther was winning favor in the eyes of all who saw her."*
>
> (Est. 2:15 ESV)

Listening to and obeying these truths lead to rendering to a higher purpose. Once we render our own personal beliefs to align with our Creator's plan, we experience:

- Our gracious God's desires to partner with Him in His mission. It is a joy to live in His will.
- Accepting that God doesn't need us in fulfilling His will, but we certainly need God as we carry out our responsibilities.
- If we don't answer God's call for bold service, He will use someone else, but we will miss out on the joy of serving.
- God's business is risky business. We take the chance of offending others by living in God's way, but it is a privilege to be a witness for Him in this world.

All throughout this narrative, we witnessed the queen maintaining her proximity to the power to deliver her people from annihilation, which she did triumphantly. She disclosed Haman's treachery to King Ahasuerus in a clever approach that allowed Haman to dig himself in a hole. It was accompanied by timing and God's mighty power and favor.

Are you allowing your ears to be filled with nonsense? Or are you allowing your ears to become sensitive to the words God is trying to give or convey to you in this timing?

Negative Effects of Not Using Your Spiritual Ears Wisely

Haman, a self-centered man, was despicable. The antagonist in the Book of Esther, he used the power of his ears to come up with plots that would destroy all Jews. In the end, his malicious plans turned out to be unfavorable for him.

Vashti knew the rules of the law, however, she allowed pride and the rebellious spirit to pronounce her from no longer being a queen. She used her ears to become deaf to following a path that was driven. In most cases, we choose to deafen our spiritual hearing from God's instruction. We entangle ourselves in the enmeshments of everyday life, when God is always guiding us using our surroundings as a mini compass. Be mindful of what you are letting yourself listen to. Is it gossip, slander, lies that are entering the gates of your ears?

I will be the first to admit I am not a big advocate for transition. But it's where God has positioned you, hidden until your appointed time. Transitions require developing the spirit that aligns us with our destiny. We all have a destiny whether we decide to intentionally participate or anticipate in lesser matters.

Esther knew the importance of her position, Esther knew that the importance of allowing her spiritual ears being a pace that led her in the right alignment could cause a turnaround. Esther valued her identity and patiently followed the instructions from God.

CHAPTER 4

The Eyes of Esther: Conflicts/Rivals

"The soul, fortunately, has an interpreter—often an unconscious but still a faithful interpreter—in the eye."

– **Charlotte Brontë, *Jane Eyre***

The sun glistened through the panels of the hallway in the entrance of the school. The golden rays made my eyes squint. It was dismissal and everyone had made preparation for the arrival of parents. On this day, however, I was panting and sorting the children in orderly fashion along the perimeter of the hall. I gasped and gulped for air. This was not my typical normal behavior for dismissal. There was a detachment as if I was just going through the motions. I was known as the smiling face teacher who brought the snacks, embrace the students with hugs and small talks during dismissal. This day was different…I had to force a smile, more or less a grimace emerging on the surface of my golden cheeks that hurt and was tightened.

Many of the colleagues were smiling and glaring my way, but I have become familiar with that signal that meant beware or as the saying goes, "objects may not seem as they look in the mirror." Yep, that was my environment.

Deep down inside, I felt my warning! Warning! Alert internal alarm, be aware! (Something did not feel right inwardly.) My school work day has come to an end. I went back to my room to collect my belongings and exit out the school building. I walked to the car and there it was—my car window shattered. No one did not even say anything or warned me, neither my so called "coworker, we are here to support each other" crew. I mean *nada*. I knew right away what this meant. The administration decided to send a threat to me for contacting the union for their unfair and unlawful procedures. I contacted the police department to file a report. They looked and examined and said frankly to me, "Ma'am, this is not a break-in entry; this is an inside job, perhaps vengeance." Yes, right off the top of their head, that was the verdict. Meanwhile, a teacher, knowing and seeing the police examining the car—the teacher known as little Miss Nosey—just drove right by…making it too obvious. However, I secretly knew and agreed. Yet somehow, I did not want to accept this reality. Was this really happening? Why?

Tears began to drench my face while I sat in that car with broken glasses splattered on the seat and just remnants remaining in their original state in the door. These were not tears of sadness but more of tears of relief; even though I was experiencing a sorrowful moment, strength began to dwell in me. I knew that my position was blameless just like Esther.

I drew from the inner strength that was concealed inside me. I did not coward down and just let life dictate a story that was not true. I called the union and let them know about the situation. They heard it all—my ugly cry and harsh breathing, trying to get the words out clearly, yet a little anguish was seeping through. The person on the phone said, "Ms. Murden, it's okay, just cry…I'm here for you," and he just listened and once I finished crying, he gave me comforting words.

This incident, environment, and me becoming a teacher gave me the training I needed to possess the land that God prepared for me. Little did I know I had to go through a hurtful situation.

Our journey requires conflicts; if we do not have a rival, how would our story be a victorious one? Remember, we are created for life with God. We are all treasured clay. Our God, the Creator, knows the how, what, and when the conflict should occur in each of our lives. God is a strategic God. God is not wondering or saying maybe I should not have given Regina that hardship. God knows exactly what we need, and God is not there condemning us and wanting us to feel bad about our lives. We must have a godly perspective. We are not a product of our circumstances. We are a product of our choices.

Ask yourself, are you going to continue to weep over what God has chosen to entrust you with in life? Or will you accept the mission He has designed for you to tackle—not alone but with His help? Just like Esther, she decided to become fearless. As the Bible states:

> *"The king was furious as he got up from dinner and went into the palace garden. But Haman stayed to beg Queen Esther for his life, because he saw that the king had a terrible end in mind for him."*
>
> *(EST. 7:7 GW)*

Esther knew she had to be courageous enough to go against unjust circumstances that was being plotted against the Jews. Sure, she was fearful at the time, but she kept moving, knowing that she served a God whose will would see it through to the end for the interest of her people. That is what we call trust. Trust requires testing and a few rattling and ruffling of the feathers.

Esther did not fixate herself on the natural circumstances that was unfolding before her eyes. She reached for within her soul to know that the journey she was on required much faith and discipline.

Conflicts and Rivals in Esther's Story

Esther was placed in a harem with a group of feisty young virgins. They were taken into captivity to become the king's property as he chose. If Esther had decided to lose sight on her hope knowing she was called for a time like this, she could have burst into panic attacks and given up. Esther could have let her eyes led her astray to the beauty of her counterparts. Sometimes we look at others as if they received an "I got it all" reward and we are left helpless. That is not the truth. Yes, we all are not created equally. We have different eye colors, intelligence, shapes, interests, and talents. Our differences do not disqualify us to be purposeful and valuable.

Esther isolated herself from the petty talk and the beauty treatments to fixate her eyes on Christ. She is nothing without God's help. She did not let internal conflicts about her beauty subside her calling.

Another conflict mentioned in Esther's story is Mordecai vs. Haman. Haman kept his eye on Mordecai. Haman felt dishonored by the inclination that Mordecai would not bow to him. Haman sought for retaliation to destroy Mordecai and his people. He convinced Ahasuerus to issue a decree saying 10,000 talents of silver would go to anyone who would destroy the Jews (Esther 3). Mordecai not bowing to Haman was interpreted wrongly. In the Jewish custom, one was forbidden to bow to occult symbols. Haman was wearing an occult symbol on his garment. Haman took it personally, looking for accusations to attack Mordecai because of his pride being slighted.

Mordecai was never depicted as a man who was easily persuasive. Mordecai's determination was to follow through honoring God. He had courage to stand alone. As we see, doing what is right does not always make you popular. Yet, he knew that obeying God is more important than obeying people.

Mordecai disapproved of the idea to bow to Haman. Yes, Jews did bow to government authorities as a sign of respect. In Persia, the kings and officials were considered divine. Deep within, Mordecai was not about to kneel before a man he knew was overtly exhibiting an occult sign on his garment. He was not going to acknowledge him as a god.

We, too, should take a stance to not allow people, circumstances, attitudes, and relationships that are unhealthy become our god in our life. The boss on the job may be asking you to bend your moral beliefs for a higher pay grade. The people at your church may be asking you to be cliquish and do unkind deeds to others who are considered outcast. Or maybe, you are self-sabotaging yourself with unhealthy thoughts about yourself and others. Whatever the exposition could be, you are given the choice to either stand on the notion of following God's approach in handling life, or being victimized by your fleshly desires. It might require being alone, accused, or even betrayed. However, when you choose to remain blameless, you are in good standing with God.

Mordecai was not caring what others thought. He used his mouth in wailing cry to others—well, as far as the law would allow him to go, which was to the gates of the courts. Dressing in lowly clothes, sackcloth, mourning from the top of his breath. No one was allowed to enter in garments that was less desirable. Mordecai knew mourning at the gates made him get noticed by the eyes of many. He requested for a fast. Mordecai saw before his eyes that Haman plotted an unlawful conspiracy to wipe out the Jews with an approval by the high authorities.

Esther was clearly using her eyes in this situation for she noticed that her uncle was acting strangely. She even sent clothes for Mordecai to change into via the servant. Mordecai refused the articles of clothing and remained in position of obedience unto God. Would you be willing to look foolish amongst others no matter what the extent? Perhaps, right now, you have heard God has given you orders to do something that in actuality does not and will not look pleasing to the sight of man's eyes? God is not waiting on the approval of man. He is often waiting to see if you will use your trust in the most obscure situations, no matter how it may look through your natural sight. Or would you succumb to the masses of the environment that God places you in to be silent and blinded from the spiritual sight God has given you to overcome a loss, conflict, or attack? God reveals His strategies often through our eyes. When we become sensitive to accepting and saying yes to God, we are rendering our hearts for a cause that is more than ourselves. We must get over ourselves. It has never been and will never be about any of us. It is about God. We always say, "Use me, God to Your greatest capacity," but we won't move in a timely manner. We become consumed by the earthly dwellings and the communal critics. But where does this all come from? We have seen evidence in the Bible and even people in modern times do miraculous acts.

In 2009, a miraculous act took place in the Hudson River. A pilot landed a plane on the water for an emergency landing. Imagine the pilot was facing a near-death experience; a pilot who was clearly responsible for the passengers that was onboard. The pilot had to decide. A quick decision to be exact. The pilot looked beyond himself and what he was seeing and relied on the source that seemed too outlandish to us and obeyed. He landed a gigantic plane in the middle of a river and reported that all survived. Now, if you were on that plane as a passenger gasping for life, you did not have any control of the next seconds of your destiny. It relied simply on the obedience of another man's decision to not look or care about how the situation appeared physically. It was about rendering what naturally makes sense to be obedient to the spiritual assignment.

Those are the opportunities given in our lives. This life that is more than about us. It is about rendered purposes for the glory of God. How many opportunities have we let pass by us because the way the outcome looks like do not make sense. We second guess ourselves. Perhaps you have been prompted to say hello to a stranger at the store. But because you were caught up in your innuendos, that stranger committed suicide later that day. Perhaps you feel a prompting to have a daily walk with a neighbor, but you become so entangled with yourself. You decide not to because the neighbor might think you are saying they are too fat. However, God is trying to use you as a vessel to save your neighbor's soul just by introducing them to Christ.

It comes from the lack of belief in ourselves, but mostly in our Creator which lessens our self-worth. This prevents us from walking into that

Promised Land that beholds our destiny. Many are holding wondrous dreams in bondage inside themselves because of fear and doubt. Many are allowing their eyes in their present situation to keep them from leaping into that next dimension. You cannot do it without the rendering process.

Rendering is an action of giving, yielding, or surrendering to something. The process of rendering, giving, surrendering, or yielding happens through action. The action is our responsibility. The action could have a negative or a positive result. When we decide to carry out a task in hopes of a good outcome, we are rendering fears, distractions, and resistance of change to fulfill that assignment. But if we are given an opportunity and glance over it, the result becomes a negative outcome for us. Often, the opportunity becomes fulfilled through another being. The journey is not going to be smooth sailing. The opposition and turbulent attacks that coincide with accomplishing a task is going to take perseverance and grit.

Mordecai knew that perseverance is required for the saving of the people. It was not about him, not for a second. His rendering took a major action of being possibly killed or losing his status in the society. Mordecai knew this was an opportunity that comes once in a lifetime. It was detrimental to him. Mordecai sent with the servant a copy of the written decree to show to Esther. The decree was to wipe out all Jews.

What if Esther said to Mordecai, "Bruh, that's not my problem. You handle it." But Esther chose not to be presumptuous but submissive to the revelation.

Once Esther received this document. It was clearly revealed before her eyes that it was not accidental she was assigned by God to be the queen and to save her people; if not, God would surely use someone else who would get the assignment done and she would surely perish.

Esther's Internal Conflict

Esther combatted with a conflict within herself daily. The insecurities that arose in her mind. The standards for meeting the beauty of a queen. Knowing when to speak and not to speak had to be taxing for her. She had to renew her mind probably hundreds of times throughout the day. She was witnessing unlawful acts delegated through a man that was her husband whom she did not agree with.

Most of us will quickly find an excuse or fault to say why we are not capable in accomplishing a task. We tell ourselves, "I can just barely do enough to keep my head above water. I possibly am not expected to keep you afloat too." Translation: "God, I am so lazy and do not want to give an effort. But I do want to look as if I am honorable."

Unfortunately, it does not work that way. Esther became aware that in God's kingdom, much is acquired beyond yourself. She gained favor in the eyes of God because she remained in position. Everywhere Esther went, she gained favor in the eyes of others. God was protecting Esther while simultaneously dominating the course for the story to unfold.

After looking at the decree, Esther requested for a fast. She called all Jews to pray for God's help with dangerous mission. Esther was nobody's dummy. She knew the stakes had gotten high. The forces of the evil were not going to prevail in her eyes. Therefore, Esther did not act in her own hands. She began to take the action through the hands of God. Submitting and leading her people to cleanse themselves and finding approval from God struck a major shift in the story. Esther received the memo it was not about her. Period. You did not find Esther using Facebook to slander Haman and showing a picture of Haman's decree to wipe the Jews out. Esther's wisdom knew whose eyes was meant to see the decree. She understood the principle of boundaries. Sometimes, we allow too many who are not in authority become expose to see certain things that are occurring in our lives. God wants you to conceal certain things that He allows only for your eyes to see while you are going through the rendering process.

We tend to show our meals, our lovely outfit of the day, and our mood for the hour to others, when God is trying to get you to learn to guard yourself from attacks by not being too open. Timing is God's weapon in defense. If Esther had started a Facebook group with the decree too soon, the deliverance of her people would not have been served because Haman would have received the news from possibly his wife, Zeresh, who joined the Facebook group. She would be reporting to him, saying, "Look at this group, they are talking about you and your plan. What are you going to do about it, Haman?"

Of course, Haman would have shut it down in a matter of time.

Esther followed through with grace by calling for a fast. This was openly giving their hearts to God while secretly planning to derail Haman's plan. So, Zeresh, Haman's wife possibly did hear about or came across Esther's Facebook group that was requesting to undergo a fast and thought nothing about it. She might have thought it was just another religious Jewish act.

It was not just another Jewish act. God was in the midst of it all. Even though God is not mentioned and seemed untraceable, He was actively moving in behalf of Esther's bold action of obedience. As Esther has stated, "And if I perish, I perish" (Est. 4:16 NIV).

Conflict with the King

Esther revealed her identity after giving the word to her husband about the plan to assassinate King Ahasuerus. She was in a slight pickle. She had just requested a fast for three days and three nights. She had now endangered her life to save her people. Let's not forget…King Ahasuerus had a little streak of "cray-cray" deep down inside. He was possessive and liked for things to go according to his ways. We see in verse 4:11, Esther had not been called to go in to the king for thirty days. That is a mighty long time, and usually, you would probably be sending out an amber alert around this time for Esther was considered a young girl. We can allude to that the king was not pleased with her at the time, and he definitely forbade her to be in his presence if he had not beckoned for her.

Esther had a lot on the fence. We saw Vashti, the queen before Esther, got dethroned simply because she decided she did not want to be shown at a banquet. Now, Esther was coming with some ammunition that could possibly get herself killed. Yet, she obediently carried out the promise. She went in the king's presence anyway without any consent.

Boxing

> *"Everyone who competes in the games goes into strict training. They do it to get a crown that will not last, but we do it to get a crown that will last forever. Therefore, I do not run like someone running aimlessly; I do not fight like a boxer beating the air."*
>
> (1 Cor. 9:25–26 NIV)

This is known as discipline with a purpose—God's purpose. Shadow boxing is a practice, but the shadow does not hit back. The war for our hearts includes many battles that we encounter daily. Jesus fought the battle, though, and has secured victory over our enemy. Just like Esther trusted God enough to step forward in faith, do likewise, holding on for dear life to God—the author of our life. Let God be God and cast yourself at the throne of grace.

Life can be like boxing with yourself. We must know how to tell our offenders it is over, and it is an official TKO for them who are trying to embark on our territory.

Let's take a look at my personal experience, which was heart-wrenching and made me felt left torn at the seams. At the time, I was an innocent teacher filled with hope and desire to teach. Life threw me a curved ball, or so it appeared at first. I was tackling with the layers of hurt that was trying to leave an imprint of offenses on my heart. I had to become a brave young lady to accept that I was given a teacher mentor who despised me and plotted against me. The environment with the school officials was reckless with their contribution of being unfair. Threats? Did it hurt? Yes, but not long because I soon learned that this was only temporary, and God needed me to trust His will in this season of heartache. It felt as if I was imagining at the time with what I thought were misconceptions. My courage to contact the union gave other teachers the opportunity to make a voice about the personal situations. They, too, were quietly hurting.

It goes to show the timing of our Creator is always significant. I remained in position just like Esther and followed what God revealed with my eyes and He directed my path in a timely manner to proceed to action.

Here's the backstory…

When I first began to reveal some of the treatment to the union. They thought I was just having rookie teacher jitters. I can understand their stance on the matter, especially with the content I was sharing with them. They possibly could have thought I was exaggerating the experience until a colleague of high caliber took that plunge too. She gave the full layout of an environment that had occult activities occurring in that specific school building. If only those walls could talk. It was in that precise timing that a link was found to expose the injustice occurring in that building. If I have waited to move a minute late or too soon, the protection that was appointed by God for me would not been accurate simply because I would have been moving in my own angst and will and not God's will. It was as if we formed our secret teacher bond and we were waiting until the great reveal.

PART 2

Ingredients of Rendering

CHAPTER 5

The Heart of Esther: Trust Psalm 31:1

"Every way of a man is right in his own eyes, but the Lord weighs the heart."

(Prov. 21:2 ESV)

I remember lying in that dark room on the floor of my classroom. I remember my heart began to be filled with praise. It was literally bursting with joy. Simply, I knew the joy of the Lord is my strength. Suddenly, a little light glistened in the room. It was as if I felt God speaking to me in that moment, saying, "Daughter, I have not abandoned you."

I knew this too shall pass. I walked out the classroom feeling like that child, saying, "I'm a rubber, you're glue; whatever you say, sticks right back on you." I felt confident knowing that the backlash and evil schemes were not penetrable.

I even said to myself, "Go ahead, shoot your best shot…you got the wrong one today." My inner alter ego name KeKe came showing out.

Remember to remain calm and collected and presentable among my peers. The irony was the setting of this place, which resembled hell, became quiet, as if you could feel something was about to suddenly burst from nowhere.

Esther knew in her heart that she should stop looking at the provision of the world and place it into the hope that the Lord will provide. We see in the story of Esther that we are called to be the salt and light of the world. God needs you to not be afraid to make a stand in the place the Lord puts you. The opportunity renders victory, therefore, do not be afraid of man or the enemy.

Esther and Mordecai understood that God delivers His people, but they knew they had to take the action in their hearts. We must do God's will and not just pray and watch. Esther teaches us through her boldness to not wait for others to do exactly what can be done by ourselves. We must get engaged and enjoy the results of sharing God's purposes for mankind.

We see that God favored Esther. When Esther spent the night with the king, God caused his heart to "loved Esther more than all the women, and she won grace and favor in his sight..." (Est. 2:17 ESV).

God is in control of the heart. We see that the king's heart was in God's hand. This allowed room for miraculous outcomes. Esther had curated a courageous heart that she was willing to give up her life for the lives of her people. This gesture alone moved God in an uplifting way to make a turnaround in the situation.

In my life, my heart resembled a potsherd that was broken into pieces. As God's treasured clay, He allowed parts to crack open to allow the treasure within to shine through. Broken into many fragments simply because my strength within me depleted; simply because I was striving and wanting to have total control. I am usually good at being in control and having it my way—or so I thought. Wrong. Let's look at the following verse:

> *"Woe to the one who quarrels with his makers, a mere potsherd with the potsherds of the earth! Woe to the one who says to the one*

> *forming him, 'What are you making?' or 'Your work has no human hands?'!"*
>
> (ISA. 45:9 ISV)

This brings clarity to our roles in life. We do not have it ALTOGETHER—never. We are a masterpiece specifically made of clay that will become dismantled from time to time with cracks that mark an awakening of a new reformed structure, letting light seep through the crevices of our new transformed shape.

God wants to use each one to this extent if you are only willing to say yes. If God would come to you today, asking much acquired beyond yourself. Will your heart be in clean standing to be a vessel that can be used in a way that allows shattering change in your community (life)?

It's the hesitation within that hinders us from moving between the brink of "not being quite there yet" to "wanting to be there" in our breakthrough. I recall wanting to literally blast some people out with spiteful words. My heart was just not quite disheartened as Esther. I had to literally surrender my all and let the Creator have the rightful position to literally shatter me into pieces when I was at the point where nothing did not make sense in my life. Yet, it took this rendering of my fleshly hardened heart to remove idols and nonsense characteristics that did not bring honor to my Father.

I ask God, "Why is the process difficult? Last time I remember, I surrendered it all. Therefore, You win." I was accusing my Creator as if He had decided to place me in the write-off section. God does not give up on us. I was looking through a lens of doubt that placed my God off the throne. Trust me—nah, don't.... Trust God. The process that often looks to never-ending and slightly tormenting is a requirement to become who you are called to be in life.

I would start the process then quit, begin again...oh, then quit...then I would go to God and say, "Here I am, please use me. I am Yours." I was repeating cycles, but not committing to the process. Finally, in my heart, I said enough! The hollow drought that was carved inside my beating heart wants to live again.

I no longer wanted the selfish approach of committing to God while holding His hands. My selfish self was saying, "Okay, I'm on the team but I'm secretly holding in my other had insecurities of wanting it my way, God." This was a hindrance in my life. God eventually wants us to grow up. God wants His sons and daughters to be who they are truly called to be in His image. In my circumstances, it was the misfortune of taking the teaching route. Every one's path may be different, but the outcome is the same for us all, which is victory. We must choose to trust the process and not let go of it. Remember, we are rendering for more. We give up something for another. You just cannot render while simultaneously holding on to the things that must go in your life.

It was a warm spring afternoon. My class was in support. I was tidying the room and inputting grades in the computer. Then came little Mrs. Roots. She allowed her roots to sink deep in this unfertilized soil. When she entered a room, you just knew it was not for wishing you well. She was a Haman. She could easily smile in your face and know she was on a formidable agenda.

"Oh, Ms. Murden, how are you today?"

Aggh. No, be an Esther; be an Esther, I told myself. Sitting up, turning my body to the side to be adjacent to her body. She quickly scanned the room and me to find anything to report to the higher forces.

Just to get a kick out this situation. I knew she would be untruthful no matter what she had seen in my room. I said, "Hey, have a seat. You want to look? I was just inputting grades in the computer."

"Oh yeah," she replied.

As I sat in disbelief, she was there to spy. I did not let someone else's obscure kick allow me to lose my focus. Distraction can be dangerous. This was just a mini crucifix. Laughing this off, we all go through our mini crucifixes to receive that resurrected promise.

What could you do to turn the heart of your King? You could come to an agreement that God knows what is best. Come into His presence through prayer. In those times, you are not petitioning; instead, you are positioning your heart to allow God to talk with you. Esther requested a fast for three days. She went to her King to hear a strategy. She could have fasted for King Ahasuerus' sake. Esther's heart was conditioned to be bent to God that she requested a fast for herself.

Are you guilty of pointing the finger to others, asking God to change them? Or asking God to please change a circumstance when you should be pleading for God to change you? When you approach our heavenly Father in this manner, you are opening a heart that is ready to be rendered. God hears these types of request. You are no longer presenting an image of selfishness. You are now being spiritual. Esther died to her flesh daily. I know at times she wanted to blast out and use spiteful words just like me. Or was even tempted to eat a meal or two during that fast. Esther knew she was not doing this alone and God was with her. She wanted to honor God's will.

Are you honoring God's will with your daily habits? If not, what needs to be changed to get in the will of God?

The heart is the pacer to life. Out of the heart flows the issue of life. A cleansed or uncleansed heart is paramount to our connectedness to God? Look at Haman, a man with a heart that needed deep cleansing. A man who wanted to wipe out an entire race; full of pride, hate, judgmental, and had bigotry traits. Well, he had a heart. Haman's heart was not beating for God. He was a man that was clearly out of God's will. He ultimately condemned his fate with death while striving to plot against Mordecai. Whereas, he died from the gallows that he invested in building in hopes of Mordecai's death. Little did he know not only did he serve his death penalty, he prepared the appointed time for his preceding death.

We can look at Haman's irrationalized views to point us to the direction in our own lives. I commit to examine my heart to see if I, too, am facing a death penalty from disobedience. We all can fall short into Haman's syndrome easily. A simple alcoholic beverage from a meetup, a new credit card account, or even an anniversary gift to the hubby by partaking in a threesome. It won't hurt, right? We must continuously die to our flesh and make choices that are leading us to the cross and not astray. You need to investigate your heart and see what your Haman's syndrome is and set boundaries. Then, trust God and confess to Him.

I confessed to God that I desperately needed Him. I was afflicted with many propositions that I knew was not christened. Many call ourselves Christians, but are we showing others what it looks like? I had to fight to show what that looked like in the school God placed me in. Saying no to unhealthy sexual activities, not participating in a modern-day toga party till you passed out, and refusing participate in the daily explicit DJ worldly jams in the cafeteria for lunch time with students. Most of these concerns would be something you would not think would be a consideration when you sign a contract to be a teacher. Yet, they were training these innocent kids in a lifestyle that was not promising but formidable.

I had coworkers come to me and say, "You dress like a Christian." Or the students mention, "You are different from the teachers." Asking was I a Christian? I had to choose between being a representative for Christ with the possibility of losing my job.

You might be facing similar concerns. There is something you know you need to do, but it means abandoning your comfort zone and stepping out in faith. You know that it's God's leading, but it's hard. You don't know what the outcome is going to be. You really don't know where you will be standing at the end of it. Esther faced this dilemma too. She chose to remain in God's presence. She knew it would be at a high cost. Because Esther trusted God, she received the king's favor to walk into King Ahasuerus' presence. Through Esther's boldness in welcoming Ahasuerus, saving her people from destruction was received. Learn to trust in God assuredly. Know that He cares for you and you can rest in His perfect guidance and wisdom for your life. Esther did it simply, and it went more than well for her. You can trust just as simply and take that step of faith! Be obedient to commit to the things that God asks of you to step beyond your comfort zone and live a life of faith.

CHAPTER 6

The Hand of Esther: Obedience But Allow Fear to Keep Us Stagnant

"I will not leave you as orphans, I will come to you."

(John 14:18 NIV)

It is in your hands.

God has been placing His magnificent hands on this journey. What seemed like despair was a hidden treasure for my soul. The hands of God do not work the same as our earthly hands. A no-brainer but I needed that reminder for my current situation. As we look closely into the Book of Esther, we see that God used His hands through time. His time. Esther was given five years of grace through the divine interception from God before leading her into her calling.

The hand of God would never lead you where you should not be. In my experience in teaching, time had passed from the first experience. God released me from that school. Was I a happy camper? Yes, indeed. Little did I know that He would send me back. This time, not in the same school. My trust level grew, and I knew God was up to something. My hopes were up high. I felt as if this time around was going to be a good teaching experience. I passed the last test. Surely, it was reward time.

Esther knew that reward was surely to follow; she was a young woman determined to complete her mission. Esther's hands were relatable to accomplishing her calling—the deliverance of the Jews. She positioned her hands through prayer that gained favor in the king's sight.

Also, Esther received provision from this obedient act. As we see, she knew the exact timing to know how to plan the feast. Esther's wisdom gave her the provision to touch the golden sepulcher. This was a mighty act upon the king to allow Esther to place her hand at the top of the sepulcher. The placement of her hand gave access to the throne room. Now, she had the heart of God. For this was what Esther was created for all along. For such a time as this. Just like Esther, are you willing to make a stance for a time as this? Are you willing to stand as a church to support the Christianity morals for such a time as this?

Therefore, I was asked by God am I willing to complete the mission, for such a time as this. My response was, "Here's my hand, lead me as you please." His hand led me right back into the classroom. This time was different, yet with familiarity. God provided me a period of grace or a time to rest for preparation to receive my authority from Him. I have not yet received that authority in my last teaching site.

At first, I was reluctant. I did not want to go anywhere near a school door. However, there was an anticipation within me. I received a call one summer evening to consider teaching for the upcoming school year. I went to the teaching site and was hired on the spot.

The emotions inside was surreal. In partiality, I questioned myself, *Regina, are you really signing up for this again?* Then the other part of me was leaping with joy as if I knew that God placed me here for an assignment.

This was the promotion season. I did not know this at the time. God will sometimes put you in places that you might not have an inkling of where you are headed. I'm here to tell you that's great. It's okay not knowing where you might be headed in the process of you simply saying yes.

Imagine, Esther had no clue of how the outcome was going to unfold. Surely, she was weary at times.

We all know in Esther's story that she stepped into victory for many. The same for you when you decide to take the risk and dive into the opportunities God presents to you.

We see how God turned the authority from King Ahasuerus, an ungodly man, to His hand by placing it in the hands of a godly woman.

There I sat at the teacher's desk in hopes for a good school year. Signs and more signs were seeping through. I saw but then did not let the signs creep into my innermost being's thoughts just yet. This time is different for me! God is protecting and leading me to victory.

Well, let's say I entered another round of saga. This level was more intense. As the saying goes, "a new level, a new devil." I was more equipped and gained wisdom from the past experience. Ironically, I entered an extremely toxic environment. There was this lady who was known as the Nazi. I was to work for her but was not quite sure how to work. She had a record for taunting people, making them restless, and an aim to terminate their teaching careers. She was vicious.

I did not understand. Why this again, but worse! *God, did I fail you? What am I doing wrong? I have not done anything wrong.* At the time, I did not know God was training and growing me for what was to come. I felt as if I was dealt lemons and more lemons. There was no way to make any lemonade out of this circumstance.

This time, the attacks came from the administration and the kids. I felt blindsided and unarmored. I did not quite understand the culture of this school. Would I be relatable?

The Haman in this assignment used time as their weapon. You were watched everywhere you could imagine. This Haman had little minions brainwashed and walked through to report every little detail that did not seem comprehensible. This was the same war but required a different strategy.

On the first day of school, I should have known this was a peculiar place. The head lady's next in charge—who just welcomed me into the school, I might add—quit on the first day of school. Red flag. I just did not yet equate the situation I have entered.

At this point, I have become submissive to the leading of my feet and spirit. Little did I know there was more work to be done with my hands in the field of teaching. So, I made up my mind to take on the task. Preparing the lesson and setting the room for instruction, I heard God whisper to me, *You are not here to teach.* The first thought that came to mind was, *Well, God, why am I here? This looks like a classroom to me. I think I'm supposed to be teaching.* I am guilty sometimes of putting God in what seems to me the proper perspective. We must remember that God's ways are not like our simple minute ways. I brushed that small whisper away. However, God did not shake loose of me. The whisper was, "You are not here to teach, this is for you. I have you here for a reason. Trust me. Promotion." Then God told me to say promotion, so I said promotion to myself. I was baffled about my presence in the school, yet there was joy surging from within. Let me tell you, God was surely right. I was not there this time for teaching. I was placed in that environment for pruning for myself. It hurt but it did not stain me mentally or spiritually.

Just as we see from year seven to year twelve in Esther's story. There was a period of grace given unto Esther. I can imagine God was pruning away some things from her too. God tends to do this before we are promoted or capable to walk in full authority.

The mountains that are placed before you are your training grounds. The mountain of fear, pride, greed, idolatry, or unending attacks. The mountains are for you to climb. It will be strenuous and challenging. The result will be glorious for you, reaching the summit. Keep in mind, these mountains are spiritual. We need to equip ourselves to speak to these mountains. We speak by professing the truth. The truth is the Word. I continuously had to climb my spiritual mountain in this new school. As the mountain became steeper, I had to profess with boldness and trust that God would see me through with this task.

Ironically, mountains are formed with an alignment from the same cause. An orogenic belt develops when a continental plate crumples and is pushed upwards to form mountain ranges. There are four types of mountains: upwarped, volcanic, folded, and fault-block. The upwarped mountains are formed from the pressure that undergoes underneath the Earth's crust, pushing upward into a peak. The volcanic mountains are formed from eruptions of hot magma from the Earth's core. The folded mountain is formed by two tectonic plates within the Earth's crust pushing against each other, generating pressure sufficient for creating large mounds. The fault-block is formed by the Earth's crust being stretched and extended by tensional forces. Most mountain ranges are formed by plate tectonics. Therefore, a shift must take place in the Earth for the uprising of the formation of the mountain to form. Just like for you and me, when spiritual mountains present themselves in our lives, it requires a shift in us. That shift of the uprising within our self requires deep trust on the truth of the Word no matter how gigantic the shift. It takes the pressure, the stretching, and the forces of pushing against each other to form a mountain.

Our mountains are powerful. Our mountains are not easily defeated. What may be your mountain is your next position for an uprising for what God has in store. At times, we are required to be spiritually aggressive in our assignments.

Esther became spiritually aggressive. She touched not the side of the sepulcher; Esther boldly touched the top of the sepulcher. Esther activated her authority. We are able to walk in authority when we begin touching the top of sepulcher that are in our lives. That promise God gave you in your heart, go after it. That's how the mountains that once look massive to you begin to yield to the purpose God have for you. God does not hand over our promises. We are responsible to remain diligent and fight to access the promise God has given us.

Next, we see how the hand of God is being revealed in the story. From the year seven to year twelve there was a period of grace. Grace is given to us by God to build us up to what he has called us to do. We view the waiting season as being punished or being set to the side and to be left out. God cannot leave you out of a story where you must win. His grace is our supernatural power activator juice to get us ready for the win.

God uses that area of your life that seem not to be working well. It looks like a failure. You are right where you belong; do not reposition yourself. Here, I was placed in a season of unsuccessful teaching. It would not propel by any means. God used my incapability of not teaching effectively to prepare for a calling of teaching the truth for His name's sake. The process will never make sense. Nevertheless, it always comes together. The blind is not leading the blind. We must transfix our minds on the purpose and not on the affliction. God is sovereign. He sees all and leads you to your promise through protection. The pain is affirmation you are on the right path.

Many are probably wondering why the attacks. They seem to be setbacks. It looks like you will never make it to the top of the mountain. God never asks you to do it alone. He will lead you and hold your hand. Your finances might be in an unsettling rut, career in shambles, but we all face an enemy. Our Haman, Satan, does not see our broken vessels. Satan see the fierce you. The end product that you are pressing towards. God blinded Satan to see you in the broken state. God created us in His image, therefore, we possess the light of greatness. Satan only sees that greatness and we are receiving the attacks from the enemy to prevent us from becoming that dynamic force.

Signet Ring

We see the hand of God is turning the soil for the Jewish people for favorable conditions. In Esther, the signet ring represented power. The signet ring is mentioned twice in Esther. First, we see:

> *"The king removed his royal ring from his finger and handed it to Haman, Hammedatha the Agagite's son, enemy of the Jews."*
>
> *(Est. 3:10 CEB)*

In this exchange, we see how the enemy tries to steal our position and take our promise from us. Here, we see Haman has unlawfully received the ring from King Ahasuerus, an ungodly man at the time. He has handed the signet ring to Haman. Here, we see that the king has given over his authority to the enemy. Many of us in life are being presented to have a royal position, but we keep handing our authority over to the enemy.

The second time we see the exchange of signet ring is in Esther 8:2 (CEB): "The king took off his royal ring, the one he had removed from Haman, and gave it to Mordecai. Esther put Mordecai in charge of what Haman had owned."

When God's hand is in it, He will hand over the authority to whom it lawfully belongs to. God is searching our hearts to see if we will trust in Him to allow God to place the authority that belongs to us in our hands. Will you continue to keep your hand drawn in a fist, trying to naturally fight the resistance within your own strength? Open and release the grasp of your hand and let God place the authority in your hands. You do not have to worry if it will be stolen from you because it's been your rightful position since birth. In the hands of God, it is when He is releasing His authority over your life that you receive favor.

John 14:18 New International Version (NIV)

18 *I will not leave you as orphans; I will come to you.*

Orphaned Spirit

I recall being isolated from the world not capable of consuming the fresh breath of living securely. It was not because of the lack of love from my mom and dad. It was not the surroundings; all along, it was because of a relationship. I became too acquainted with the images of the world. The images that was developed through snapshots of smiles, togetherness, and memories. My images did not always align. Deep down within, the hurt brew the obscurities that I have not yet began to recognize. I detached myself from the darkroom. Yes, I know that sounds funny. I alienated myself from understanding how the process of being developed in a darkroom creates the picture. I only focused on the images. The images are what we perceive while not showing what has been conceived to develop what we see to be an image.

My images were friends that deserted me, school, a career, and family. It was not until I removed myself from the light reflected from the objects that I could see the personal images that occur in my life.

Not even thinking about who is the mastermind of the darkroom; carelessly, the one not being credited for the negatives of the development process in those dark spaces is God, my Creator and your Creator. I am ashamed to admit, coming from such a strong Christian family of faith, that I dejected myself to live below my rightful identity. I was an orphan. Yeah, I had my mom and dad whom I am grateful for, but I did not know my heavenly Father. In that darkroom, I was holding on to the negatives and did not grasp the process of the developer. It was not the lack of knowledge. I grew up in a Christian home and reciting prayer for others and myself. However, I struggled with what is known as the orphaned spirit. This orphaned spirit stole my peace and my reassurance in my identity. You might be asking yourself, how can that be? She definitely must have been sleeping in church. It's similar to how you could have an estranged earthly father. You know all of his characteristics, you know his birthdate, maybe even what he like and dislikes, yet you withhold your total trust from him because you feel abandon, wounded, and hurt because you do not have your earthly father in your life. That can be devastating.

I became a victim. Why me? So much what I thought to be unnecessary pressures were imparted to me. It was not fair! Until I began to really dig deep beyond the images I was seeing occur in my own life. I went to the darkroom and began to explore my negatives. What actually happened in that darkroom? I had questions for the developer. In that space, surrendering and looking at my circumstances that looked dark was necessary for my development. It was by exploring that I formed the relationship my God, the developer, wanted all along. The hurt, the abandonment was Him all along never forsaking me but inviting me to come deeper into His presence. It was not enough to just go off alone with my family's faith. I had to develop my own foundation of strong faith to fight my battles that are specifically designed for me to become a brighter image for this world to see. Going back to that darkroom allowed me to let all the shackles of that orphan spirit to vanish and I began to truly seek a life after God with trust.

I give you permission if you, too, find yourself feeling abandoned and rejected yet you truly, deep down, love God in the best way you know how. I invite you to trust God. Those divine interruptions are for your good. Lean in, just like Esther had too; trust and believe that God will take care of you. I promise He never disappoints. I am a living witness. I am now grateful for the darkrooms that I look forward to them. Do you know your Father? Do you truly know your heavenly Father? If not, it's not too late. He's waiting for you now to begin producing images through you that the world needs to see.

CHAPTER 7

The Mind of Esther: Newness of the Mind

"You have power over your mind—not outside events. Realize this, and you will find strength."

– **Marcus Aurelius**

The journey is God's idea. We allow the spirit of fear to hinder us from becoming the person God called us to be and do the things He called us to do. Do not tolerate the spirit of fear. Fear is conniving and often leads you to the path of isolation. When you are isolated outside the will of God, you are allowing the enemy to paralyze you in moving into that ordained assignment.

The mind is our battlefield. We are called to renew the mind daily. The schemes and exposure to ideas can distract us and get us off the course we are meant to tread.

The enemy had convinced King Ahasuerus that the Jewish people were aliens and needed to be exiled. The renewal of the mind requires continuous discipline to watch over your spoils. The king allowed a hold of the schemes of the attack from the enemy to seep into his mind to think that a nation of people could cause harm and would be hostile to him. Sometimes we give authority to others without realizing the consequences. This seems to be the case here. Little did he know that Queen Esther was a Jewish and would be slaughtered like the others if Haman's wicked plan succeeded.

Our minds can lead or keep us from the treasures that lie ahead. To trust in rendering means my mind must become stable to receive God's guidance. We boldly shake off the spirits of confusion and double-mindedness.

The enemy will use the current situation you are in. He would allow you to question your beliefs and the way life appears in the natural, removing the confidence that is rooted in your mind to be replaced with fear and doubt.

Trusting is more than saying the words. Trusting is relying on the Word while doing the work that is required of you. Many are not rendering because they have believed that we serve a God who is magical and grants wishes. Therefore, we are not seeing the manifestation of lives because of the false connotation. We lose hope in ourselves when the hope should have been placed in God. Our misconception of God allows unbelievers to not understand our reason for serving Him. We have unconsciously aborted the rendering process that captures the ones who are uncertain about their faith.

In the story, the king did not take the time to find out more details. This would have prevented the calamity of the attack of the throne. We, too, like King Ahasuerus, are guilty of not taking the effort to investigate the details of our life.

Self-reflection….

We are here. Okay, but why? You have a deep desire to pursue certain interest. Why? You are going through the unusual havoc in your life. But why?

We fail to get the details. Without the reasoning, we will never know the ultimate "why." When we become victims of this mentality, we are losing our positions. God wants us to be alert. We serve a God who does not believe in complacency.

In this place of my employment, the new administration had set a precedence that everyone should fear their roles. This spirit of idolatry has become blatantly unlawful. Many teachers became fretful, disillusioned, and yes, quit for the tyranny that overflowed into the professional and personal lives. We were being trained to bow unhealthily to the leader.

When you place yourself on the throne, we pervert the process of rendering for more. This administrator became delusional in the state of mind to believe they ruled the lives of the teachers.

God does not give anyone the authority to manipulate others into unhealthy choices. I found myself in this sickening environment. I had to decide to trust God despite what I was seeing in the natural to ignite the power from the supernatural.

Yes, I did not become oblivious to the surroundings. I remain faithful to knowing that if I remain obedient and in position to the purpose I was called to at this appointed time, I would be protected.

Mordecai and Esther renewed their minds for a higher purpose. Esther had to guard her heart and what her eyes had seen to progress with her assignment. We see in the story: "Mordecai prayed to the Lord, calling to mind what the Lord had done in the past…" (Est. 4:18 GNTA).

Mordecai knew the importance of praying back the promises to God. This displayed belief and confidence for a breakthrough for the Jews.

When you find yourself in an unfavorable situation? Pray back to God the promises by keeping in memory how you will remain as a faithful servant.

I found myself in the classroom or lunch break in the car. Praying back the promises of how God is so faithful to my concerns. I brought back to mind the memories of the times He delivered me from the previous school scandals. I know this too; He will come through.

This time around, I had a little pep in my step because, well, it was a new devil for a new level, but with the same type of personality—pathetic. I walked around with joy inside. Many could not understand how I was able to muster up any joy in such a dismal place. I remembered that my external circumstances do not affect my mind. The joy of the Lord is our strength. Once we become true warriors in believing this truth. We are armored to fight any monster coming our way: boogie man, war wolfs, and even cookie monster himself. I have come to the actualization no one would barge in and take the treasure that belonged to me. I was not going to be afraid and become wimpy in a corner and say, "Okay, you can have it," when it was not theirs in the first place. So, that's right; now I want my cookie back that the cookie monster stole from me.

We see that Mordecai and Esther became fearless beings. They did not lose their dignity, integrity, or holiness. They remained in the presence of God. When God see that we are fearless, we want out in a way without Him doing the work for us only. He blows our mind.

King Ahasuerus had an act down that was godly and positioned the timing of deliverance. He reminisced about the time in his mind when Mordecai brought up the accusation of a plot to assassin the king. The king's memory revealed he did not rightfully reward Mordecai. God's timing is best. He allowed the favor to be upon Mordecai when suitable by placing the seed in the heart of Ahasuerus to reward Mordecai's previous deed.

There are seeds we sow that we may not harvest when we expect it. The seeds always grow at the precise timing of God. Esther did not find her mind under siege of being confused. She could easily have fallen for the demise schemes of the enemy. She did find herself going wayward—"Oh, I think God sent me," or "I think I might save the Jews." She was a ferocious fighter who remained faithful.

CHAPTER 8

The Mouth of Esther: Transparency (to Love Others Fully)

"One's eyes are what one is, one's mouth is what one becomes."
– John Galsworthy

My mouth can get me in trouble. I sometimes need a muzzle for the outbursts that are ungodly. Sometimes finding fault in others saying, "She shouldn't have sat by me," "She made me say that," or "They knew not to mention that." The list of excuses continues to bombard the main reason. I need to keep my big mouth shut. Speak only when necessary.

I have not overcome this area in my life. This is my major weakness. I falter with the mouth. I admire how Esther was able to keep her mouth close.

I would love to sit down with her and ask her, "What's the trick to keeping your mouth shut?" Come on, surely Esther was thinking some absurd and provoking thoughts in her mind. Yet she still managed to keep her mouth shut.

I truly believe Esther had come to a point in her life where she became a servant to the purpose and not just merely believing the call assigned to her. She literally died to her fleshly desires. That is not easy. I catch myself in the car driving on the highway. I begin looking to the left and the right of me. There goes my big mouth. All sorts of judgmental comments.

So, I'm like Lord—my mouth is loose. I just cannot help it. C'mon. Then a whisper to me resonates inside: *You can help it. You just do not want to grow to the maturity of discipline to remain silent when acquired.* Truthfully that is my reason. He'll say, "Look ahead and keep driving." Then I would follow the order of my God. I do not want to deliberately disobey. I just have the slips of the tongue. I will continue on the course of my destination, looking ahead as instructed by God. Before I know it, I have fallen again with the tongue. Someone driving too slow in front of me, or a driver cut too short on my side transitioning lanes. I begin to murmur and complain. I know better. Well, why won't I just do the right response?

Our habitual actions become part of us. We need to become stronger than the habits that could be hindering our growth as a person. For we all know the power of the tongue—death and life is in that little pink sword that darts in and out of your mouth.

I have really gone to the extent—here, God, take my tongue; it's yours. Reading self-help books, including that dandy book called *30 Days to Taming Your Tongue*. Good stuff really is until I begin to feel guilty for all the wrong things I do with my tongue, intentionally and unintended.

I've tried the silent treatment. I would not even speak much. Just a few words such as yes, no, I don't know to others. Well, the longevity of that state of mind was short-lived—as short as six hours at the most. It was a major flop because I managed to say even more than I had beforehand because of all the verbiage that built up over the time I was barely speaking. I was a motor mouth and a train wreck.

Yet we can look at Esther and how she remained her position in silence. She came to the point where she was able to submit and say with the rendering of her heart: "Father, not my will but Your will be done." When you submit the tongue, God can use you. You have God's heart because you are showing that you are mature to the level where you can render your personal beliefs to become God's mouthpiece. God is searching for mouthpieces. Will you be that piece that God needs to complete the whole story for His kingdom? He is calling us for His name's sake.

Esther's lips was sealed in that harem of ladies. She kept gossip from the crevices of her lips. Esther portrayed courageous strength to keep silent around the king. And most importantly, Esther understood her hidden season was required to get to the releasing of her destiny. Through her hidden season, not broadcasting her Jewish origin, Esther gained the strength of patience to know that in a time as this, God will do the revealing. She was placed in the center of the Persia to access of information, yet Esther remained hidden in her silence.

God knows silence is not a punishment. But if we open too soon, we could jeopardize our blessing and bring about curses. God expects us to be willing vessels that are broken to experience a duration of change that require the giving up of the comforts of our fleshly desires.

The mouthpiece of Esther led to triumph. When she mentioned to about the king and being summoned. In chapter four of Esther:

> *"And Hathach went and told Esther what Mor'decai had said. Then Esther spoke to Hathach and gave him a message for Mor'decai: 'All the king's servants and the people of the king's provinces know that if any man or woman goes to the king inside the inner court without being called, there is but one law; all alike are to be put to death, except the one whom the king holds out the golden scepter that he may live. And I have not been called to the come in to the king these thirty days.' And they told Mor'decai what Esther had said. Then Mor'dcai told them to return answer to Esther, 'Thing not that in the king's palace you will escape any more than all the other Jews. For if you keep silence at such a time as this, relief and deliverance will rise for the Jews from another quarter, but you and*

> *your father's house will perish. And who knows whether you have not come to the kingdom for such a time as this?"*
>
> (Est. 4:9–14 RSV)

We see that Esther was ushered into her appointed time to speak for her identity. A mouthpiece is used for transparency. Esther was about to provide her testimony with the possibility of losing her own life for the sake others. Here in Esther's prayer in chapter four, we see the pleading of getting the permission to speak from her God first by placing Him as a just Lord in her life.

> *"From birth, I have heard among my people that you, Lord, chose Israel from among all nations, and our ancestors from among all their forebears, as a lasting inheritance, and that you fulfilled all your promises to them. But now we have sinned in your sight, and you have delivered us into the hands of our enemies, because we worshiped their gods. You are just, O Lord."*
>
> (Est. 4:16–17 NABRE)

Our prayer is our sweet supplication to God. We honor God when we come with praise and thanksgiving. We dishonor God by only seeking the petitions of our hearts.

Our words create our atmosphere. If you complain a lot, the environment is surrounded with negative vibes. If you exuberantly praise, your surrounding is filled with lightheartedness. The mouth is the weapon of defense from the snares that strike us in life.

Esther had set her atmosphere before touching that scepter through the linguistic art: "Lord, do not relinquish your scepter to those who are nothing. Do not let our foes gloat over our ruin but turn their own counsel against them and make an example of the one who began this against us" (Est. 4:22 NABRE). She acknowledged that she needed the mercy of God.

Esther used her wisdom in orchestrating the outcome. She spoke with confidence: "'If it pleases the king,' replied Esther, 'let the king, together with Haman, come today to a banquet I have prepared for him'" (Est. 5:4 NIV). The king came to an agreement and summoned Haman. Clearly, Esther had learned the habits of her husband. She knew from previous experience Vashti had shamed him. This time, she preserved the dignity of her king and created a more suitable setting to reveal her concerns.

Regardless, we know that Esther did not make her transitional move during the first feast. Yes, she had created an atmosphere that was pleasing to the king. She had learned the importance of patience. She still remained silent. Esther's act had to be selfless, for her people could have been killed on the spot. Her assignment was not attached to herself. Others was attached to the assignment. Ahasuerus enjoyed himself, and he was moved to ask Esther again what her petition might be. Was this now the time to speak? This is where the drum roll begins. Imagine you are given to use your mouth to request and tell all at that very moment. But Esther chose not to speak. Are you kidding me? I would definitely have failed. I would have spilled the beans about everything. Esther's composure of patience granted the blessing of God. True obedience requires us to do what God says when He says it. Our obedience is an expression of love to our God. Esther showed God she loves Him more than anything, and she's willing to wait on His perfect timing to move and not when it suited her. In the delay is the promise. At the second banquet, Esther was released to speak for her people. God had filled her with the right words to convince Ahasuerus about Haman's deeds. The transparency of Esther revealing she was Jewish gave her the opportunity to save her people. The king had become admirable of Esther and did not want to commit to an act that would defile Esther and her people. God will do that with our mouthpieces to bring about our testimony to others.

Words can shape our environments into one with undesirable conditions. Haman is an example of someone presenting a doom state in his life. In God's eyes, nothing goes unnoticed. He sees all. Haman had a rectifying day. It had come. Little did he know that the works of his flesh had built the gallows and led him to his defeat. Our atmosphere cultivates are outcome. God wants us to be ready before the breakthrough happens. If you are seeking relocation, you prepare for moving. If you are seeking for leadership, then you shall place yourself as a pupil. God honors our surroundings that we create. He honored Haman's too. Be careful how you use your words; it could cause you to lose an opportunity for God's name. Mordecai understood, for he told Esther it was time to speak. If she did not, God was going pass her by to get the job done. What are you not rendering that could be holding from your appointed time?

When the king asked Haman, what would you request to do from an official of God standing with the king? He pronounced the fate for Mordecai. He spoke to the mountain that represented the colliding forces of the two—Mordecai and Haman. Haman spoke his ruins.

God will position your enemies to speak their fate. Their unhealthy deeds are setting up an atmosphere that is defeating for them. They have not rendered for the purpose other than for themselves.

CHAPTER 9

The Crown of Esther: God Never Puts a Crown on a Swollen Head

"My crown is called content, a crown seldom kings enjoy."

– William Shakespeare

We all envision God saying, "You get a crown. You all get a crown." But without the works, what the does the crown represent? God never puts a crown on a swollen head. Could your ego be delaying you from receiving the crown?

Esther, a young lady, knew that the crowning of Jesus brought righteousness into her life. We are caught looking at others that we even want their crowns as well. We leave from carrying our own crown that we allow it to become tarnished. We cannot be weary from meddling with other's affairs and expect to get a title.

We look at the title and become obsessed with the idea of what God is trying to offer. We do not focus on the role or tasks to obtain the title. The role usually requires work. God wants you moving. His movement entails from the inside out. Whereas He is willing to remold your character to give you the restoration.

I was so upset, frustrated, and scornful at times. I saw He was leading me to victory. I became obsessed with the title and not the role. I lost the sight of the workmanship of my King whom I serve. I do not want you to make the mistakes that I attained through my own efforts and wishes. My head was still a little too swollen for God to use me.

My appointed time has not presented itself.

When we come to our senses that it's no longer us but all Christ, we have rendered. Through our pain, we find God. As for God, He is asking you to render your heart to Him. God knows once you get the crown, the exposure of the little nuances that He is trying to get rid of within your soul will be heightened.

When the time presents itself, would you be ready? God's crown is not like a man-made crown. His crown comes with thorns, sacrifices, rendering of your heart.

Perhaps your heart has become so hardened and He will not be able to use you because you have become tasteless to God.

Esther's thorn was the silencing of her identity that she was a Jew. She had been an orphan her entire life. She did not belong to anyone as a little girl and the identity crisis did not get any better as she grew older. She could not even say whom she belonged to in the presence of her husband. Of course, that thorn hurt Esther. She wanted to get rid of the tormenting ordeals that followed her as she carried that thorn. Your thorn may be different, but are you willing to coexist with that thorn to get your position for that appointed time?

Jesus even knew timing was the essence to receive the crown from the heavenly Father. We see at the cross that Jesus, too, begged for His Father to remove the cup from Him if it is His will. The time for us to render is crushing and piercing our flesh.

Do not let fashion, a luxury car, or even a person allow your crown to be tarnished. Let's flip it for a minute—the story of Esther could have been a devastating story. Once Esther received the title of being a queen, she could have had sulked in the lavishness—the best fragrances, consuming the best garments. She could have become a walking reality TV star, treating the people of the court lowly as she elevated herself with the crown of misery.

The flesh wants the earthly possessions. The spirit requires the discipline and connection with God to thrive. When we do not submit and bow before our King, before the throne, we miss the treasures He is placing inside us.

Before I was taught, I was a sheltered and a weakling Christian girl who lack exposure to the society. God knew He gave me my crown before the expected time. It would fall right off. It would not have a great value of significance. The irony of receiving the crown takes time. For some, it takes months, years, even decades, depending on the necessities of the training field God has predestined for you. Of course, it also depends on how willing are we to learn and pass to the next mastery skill.

The stewardship that Esther depicts with her talents and spiritual gifts are recommendable. We all are called to steward our emotions, the tasks at our jobs, and yes, our mouths. My mouth gets me every time. I am not a gossiper, but I sure can be judgmental and that is not a quality meant for receiving the crown.

The essence of being content shows how we trust God right where He has us. You may not have that family, dream job, or house on the hill, but do you have a heart that God can use? When God sees that you can authentically render your broken heart that has been shattered to Him, the shifting happens, and when it does, you will be prepared.

My obedience to go back to the school gave me a short-term mission this time around. I only went through the turmoil for a semester, but it felt like forever. Perhaps, if I had stayed longer, I might have had a nervous breakdown. God honors our obedience. Me walking through the halls of disarray but at the same time praising God and walking with joy positioned me with my enemy. This thorn was a gift given to me that I could never purchase. I became content knowing that God was up to something that did not involve me. I was over myself. It was not about what I wanted or so-called what I thought I needed.

This time around, God placed me in a group. A private group. A community of support. The irony is God used this group of people who knew about the terrain of this mountain better than I knew myself. He used my ears and my heart to know the timing of the movement. When you are in step with God, God will give the provision of the tools to lead you out of that wilderness. This wilderness led me today to writing. A calling that seems to be beyond my sight, far-fetched. My God gave me a burden to carry to help deliver others who may be struggling with their route in life. They are struggling with trusting God. It seems to never end. You feel as if you are being punished. I am here to encourage you to hold on. Do not give up your crown for someone else to wear. The bigger the crown, the heavier the burden. God is just waiting on you to render that heart to Him. You were never called to carry it yourself. He is the teacher and you are the pupil. Abide in His ways and His strategies. God is forever faithful.

Steps to Obtaining the Crown

Communication – The gift of language should not be used for slandering purposes. It should be used for guidance and praise and in forming a relationship with Christ and the people He brings into your proximity.

Read – Reading is good. Learn about what God is trying to teach you in this current season. The preparation is valuable when you receive the crown. You must read your Bible to know what is next. I have not seen anyone who just rely on themselves become unstoppable.

Action – This requires not just moving your mouth and you naming and claiming it in Jesus' name. This is not the way to allow God to truly use your heart in a way that will render for the body of Christ. You cannot give up or stop moving. Even Jesus keeps moving. He rests for a little while, but He keeps moving. Make sure you are moving about your Father's purposes and not just moving out of busyness. Laziness is a clever strategy that the enemy tries to use on us to prevent us from getting the crown that God has for us. He makes you become comfortable and sulk in your emotions. Before you know, your fight has been replaced with complacency and you are not moving progressively in God's will.

Get Uncomfortable – If you are not challenging yourself to feel intensified, you are doing life wrong. Being a risk-taker captures the heart and hand of God. Take that leap of faith. God will not let you fail. He holds true to His promises and allows what He assigns to you to come to pass in due time.

Don't be a Vashti and lose your crown; be an Esther and wear the crown of victory.

CHAPTER 10

Rendering of the Heart

"Always render more and better service than is expected of you, no matter what your task may be."

– Og Mandino

Rendering brings wisdom, restoration, and stretching of faith. My journey was met with a lot of heartfelt tears. God never let go of me. The bashing from others for no apparent reason made me become a vessel that could be used for more. My assignment was attached to others.

By me going to the teacher's union, I spoke out the treatment that was not validating. This bold step allowed freedom for other teachers to feel open to want to express their hurt. My obedience led to the hurt of other teachers.

It was no accident that Esther, a Jew, was selected as queen. It was God's doing. And if she decided not to address the king, God would find someone else, but she would miss out on the opportunity to be of service to the Lord and His people.

For we are all created for a time as this—conflict, mourning, and eventually celebration. Refuse to go another day rebuking the resistance that God has placed in your life today. Embrace your hurt—there lies your treasure. A rendered heart can capture so many souls for God.

Do not miss your opportunity. God is waiting for you to allow Him to resurrect your heart, removing that bitterness, unforgiveness, and self-doubt, so that you can be who you are created to be all along in such a time as this.

Betrayal will come, but the spirit of fear does not have to take residence in your heart. You must obtain the spirit of boldness for deliverance. Esther revealed the plot to destroy her and her people, then dramatically named the mastermind: "This wicked Haman!" (Est. 7:6 ESV).

In our day, this is sometimes cast as the difference between using explicit language of faith in public. For instance, if called on to open a city council meeting with prayer, do we use generic "God" language, or do we pray "in the name of Jesus Christ"? Esther may represent the choice to refrain from flaunting God's electing choice of Israel at a time when the surrounding culture was newly opened to this community in their midst. At the same time, Esther offered a distinct understanding of the relation between God's action and human obedience.

Are you pleading daily for the people who are assigned to you? Remember, God has not and will not abandon you.

God brought Esther into royal dignity. He will honor the same position for you, too.

CHAPTER 11

Rendered for More: My Story

This section may allow you to evaluate which parts you are surrendering to God and the parts you may be holding on to in life. Use this as a supplementary guide as you read.

Introduction

What should I render? Include specifics. How long have I been holding on to my heart's desires? What are my feelings about surrendering wholeheartedly to God?

Chapter 1

In what ways am I rushing through the process? What false impression is hindering my growth to letting go? Do I really believe that God's provision is enough for me?
False Impression: I know God is mighty but I'm not sure I am good enough for Him to work in my life.

False Impression: Everyone seems to hear from God. I must not be working hard enough.

These are a few. What are some false impressions in your life that may have you hesitating that God wants to make imprints in your life? Jot them down.

Chapter 2

What steps could I take to show God that I trust Him more? Do I wander or rest in His presence? What does my spirit reveal about me when I encounter others? Write about a recent experience with someone. What was your reaction?

Chapter 3

Begin by praying:

"What shall I render unto the Lord for all his benefits toward me? I will take the cup of salvation, and call upon the name of the Lord. I will pay my vows unto the Lord now in the presence of all his people."

(Ps. 116:12–14 KJV)

Practice to listen with your ears. Watch how you will begin to see more of God's whispers in your life through the daily relationships you encounter.

Look inwardly and see how there are ways you can allow God to bring shifts of change in your life.

Chapter 4

So, what are your eyes saying about you? Perhaps, you are self-absorbed. You have not given it a second thought to look up. Maybe you are overlooking and straining your eyes and just need to transition the vantage point of your view to look at the whole picture God is trying to reveal.

What is your response when you begin to feel the prompting of God, telling you to move to see the newness He is trying to present in your life? Do you resist change? Are you holding on to the past and refusing to open your eyes to see the opportunities of the future?

Chapter 5

Where do you seek shelter? Is your heart overly consumed by the pressure of the world? Or have you been able to stop to listen to the rhythm of your heart? List ways you use to fight the enemies' schemes to distract you from listening to a place of rest. When was the last time you listen to your heart?

Chapter 6

Can you think of anyone God has placed in your life to be His hand? How have they helped you? Write a prayer to help you acknowledge the hands He has placed for such a time in your life.

Chapter 7

How do you fight your battles? Do you allow the voices in your head to overshadow the truth that is spoken over your life?

If so, what could you do to reposition your stance against the enemy's snares?

Chapter 8

This is war. Yes, I get it! This war we combat daily is won by peace. What words are you speaking over yourself lately? Are they triumphant or dishonorable?

Word #1

Word #2

____

____

Word #3

____

____

Chapter 9

What have you seen personally in your life that makes you feel that you are worthy of living a crown-fulfilled life?

____

Chapter 10

Below, write your own belief statement, proclaiming why you will trust God in such a time as this. How I will relinquish my perception of a life that God wills for me? Use this belief statement as a reminder to be bold to submit the unwanted characteristics that are not Christlike.

____

____

____

Q&A

What part of Esther do you possess?

Do you often get frustrated after going through circumstances that do not go as you expected?

a) Yes b) No, hardly ever. c) Sometimes
d) Yes, when my expectations are high. e) Never

Do you move suddenly when often prompted with a task to attempt?

a) Yes b) No c) Sometimes
d) Never e) I have no clue.

Do you like being around a lot of people?

a) Yes b) No c) Sometimes
d) I must be in a mood for people. e) Never

How do you enjoy conversation?

a) Always b) Seldom c) Occasionally
d) Never e) Only with myself.

Do you meditate? If so, how regularly?

a) Yes, at least once a week. b) Yes, at least three times a week.
c) No d) I would like help. e) I only meditate when I sleep.

Are you forgiving?

a) Yes b) Yes, more than others. c) Sometimes
d) Never e) What does that mean?

Do you blurt out what comes to mind or do you process your thoughts first?

a) Yes always. b) Yes, only in defense. c) Sometimes
d) Never e) Does social media count?

Do you see yourself drained often?

a) Yes, more than usual. b) Yes, occasionally. c) No
d) Never e) I avoid mirrors at all cost.

Are others consumed by your complaining?

a) Yes, every day. b) Yes, occasionally. c) Randomly
d) Never e) Does being a female give me leverage?

Are you a giver?

a) Yes, daily. b) Yes, occasionally. c) Yes, seldom.
d) No, I don't have time. e) I like to receive.

Do you enjoy receiving from others?

a) Yes, always. b) Sometimes c) Rarely d) No, never.
e) I feel guilty when I receive from others.

Do you notice the subtle things in your surroundings?

a) Yes, always. b) Yes, sometimes. c) Yes, if it's valuable to me.
d) Never e) Duh, I have eyes.

Do you consider yourself loyal?

a) Yes b) Yes, when I choose to be. c) Rarely
d) Never e) Who cares about loyalty?

Are you secretive?

a) Yes b) Sometimes c) More than others.
d) Never e) Not today.

Do you complete most task?

a) Yes b) Sometimes c) Rarely d) Never
e) Depends what is considered a task.

Do you think about the pros and cons before deciding?

a) Yes b) Sometimes c) Seldom d) Never
e) I am a dear relative to the tin man.

If your friend invites you to hang out, how often do you hang out with them?

a) Always b) Sometimes c) Rarely
d) Never e) Does in my head count?

Do you take a long time primping?

a) Yes b) Sometimes c) Rarely
d) Never e) I must be selfie ready.

Do you talk more than you listen?

a) Yes b) Sometimes c) Rarely
d) Never e) Depends on the person.

Do you enjoy preparing meals? Or would you prefer eating the meal?

a) Enjoy preparing meals mostly.
b) Enjoy preparing meals sometimes.
c) Enjoy eating the meal more.
d) Enjoy both
e) Don't have time for that...Uber Eats, please.

Are you adventurous?

a) Yes b) Sometimes c) Occasionally
d) Never e) No way!

Add up your score: a=1, b=2, c=3, d=4 e=0

Descriptors:

Mindful One (0-11)

You are probably one tha uses self- talk for mind awareness. You seem to be away maybe engulf your thoughts more than your surroundings. That's okay when a problem needs solving. You are usually the go to person that have resourceful methods for most difficulties.

Spiritual Eyes Seeker (12-24)

You are the one that see all and does not miss a thing. You do not only see others for face value. Yet, you are capable to see what relies within others. You are a great companion in having for fresh eyes to settle conflicts and bring ideas that are edgy and rewarding for all.

Open Ears (25-35)

You the person that serve best from listening to others stance. You don't make a move to quickly until you heard all the sides to a situation. Then you execute. When you execute you are dynamite!

Mighty Mouth (36-41)

Let the chatter begin! Many believe you are the one that may not always have a clear perspective. Your mouth carry weight. You are bold with a purpose and uses words eloquently. Sometimes when touched emotionally in an upsetting way. Your approach can be harsh but you do not intentionally mean to be wrongful.

Restful Spiritual One (42-47)

You are cool cucumber. You serve with tranquility. Always soaking up others energy fuels you in making decisions in life. You are not to overlooked. Sometimes your calmness comes off as weakness. In actuality, it is your strength that keeps you prevailing.

Warrior Walker (48- 53)

You are the one that never sitting still. You are on the move. You travel with purpose in mind. You tread softly when needed and move with a force when least expected. You serve by giving time to others and connecting the pieces to a story. Simply because you have traveled many places in your life spiritually, physically and mentally.

Scoring

0-11

It's okay. You are just getting started and becoming in tune with your strengths.

12-24

All eyes are on you. You are walking into your purpose with 20/20 spiritual vision.

25-35

Alright! I see you. You are one to not be reckon with. You are all ears.

36-41

Oh yeah, you are talking yourself right into victory.

42-47

Rest assured you bring calmness to the atmosphere. You are not going to bring and drama.

48-53

You are the one to walk with when times are troubled.

Notes

"Characterizing Esther from the Outset: The Contribution of the Story in Esther 2:1–20." 2019. Jhsonline.Org. http://www.jhsonline.org/cocoon/JHS/a093.html.

"Definition of Rendered | Dictionary.Com." 2019. www.dictionary.com. https://www.dictionary.com/browse/rendered.

Coffman, James Burton. "Commentary on Esther 3:4." *Coffman Commentaries on the Old and New Testament.* https://www.studylight.org/commentaries/bcc/esther-3.html. Abilene Christian University Press, Abilene, Texas, USA. 1983--1999.

Moore, Beth. *Esther: It's Tough Being a Woman – Bible Study Book.* (Nashville: Lifeway.Com, 2019). https://www.lifeway.com/en/product/esther-bible-study-book-P005162885.

"Esther Bible Timeline". 2019. Biblehub.Com. https://biblehub.com/timeline/esther/1.htm.

"Inspirational Quotes (55264 Quotes)." 2019. Goodreads.Com. https://www.goodreads.com/quotes/tag/inspirational.

Swindoll, Charles R. *Perfect Trust.* (Nashville: Thomas Nelson, 2012).

"Esther." *Matthew Henry Commentary on the Whole Bible (Complete).* Bible Study Tools. https://www.biblestudytools.com/commentaries/matthew-henry-complete/esther/.

CPSIA information can be obtained
at www.ICGtesting.com
Printed in the USA
LVHW090130180420
653845LV00002B/2/J

9 781400 331093